ST
UPRIGHT

STANDING UPRIGHT

DEFENDING YOUR FAITH WITHOUT OFFENDING YOUR NEIGHBOR

SANDY MALCOM

TATE PUBLISHING & Enterprises

Published by Tate Publishing & Enterprises, LLC
127 E. Trade Center Terrace | Mustang, Oklahoma 73064 USA
1.888.361.9473 | www.tatepublishing.com

Tate Publishing is committed to excellence in the publishing industry. The company reflects the philosophy established by the founders, based on Psalm 68:11,
"The Lord gave the word and great was the company of those who published it."

Book design copyright © 2010 by Tate Publishing, LLC. All rights reserved.
Cover design by Rebekah Garibay
Interior design by Lindsay B. Behrens

Published in the United States of America

ISBN: 978-1-61739-247-4
1. Religion / Christian Life / Personal Growth
2. Religion / Christian Life / General
10.11.16

DEDICATION

This book is dedicated first and foremost to my wife Sarah. Without her support and love, I could not even attempt such a task as this. I thank her for staying with me through the long years of my growing up. She has always offered me her full support on my many endeavors. Whatever success they have produced, I credit to her.

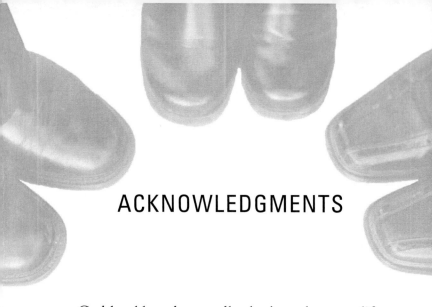

ACKNOWLEDGMENTS

God has blessed me endlessly throughout my life. One of the most amazing examples is my wife Sarah. When I started dating her, just after I had graduated high school, I just thought that she was a beautiful, fun person to be with. It took me a lot of growing up to realize how much more there was to this woman God had placed in my life. Without her, there is no telling where I'd be or what rock I'd be living under. She is a continual inspiration to me.

My daughter Elise has made me so proud, and I thank God for her every morning as I pray. She told me once that she liked living in the small town we live in because she liked to be known as Sandy

Malcom's daughter. I can't explain how proud that statement made me feel and how it inspired me to be a better person.

I thank the members of Harmony Baptist Church for being the Christian people that they are and loving my family over the years. It is truly our home.

I thank Tate Publishing for having faith in what I'm trying to say.

TABLE OF CONTENTS

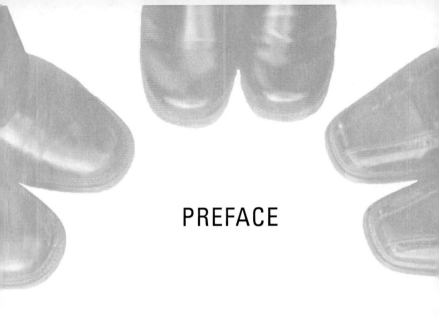

PREFACE

When I buy a book, I'm usually eager to get started reading it. When I open it the first thing I do is thumb through the pages of the preface, just to see how long it is. I hate the preface; however, in the interest of being able to say that I finished the book, I find it necessary to endure it. Although, I'd almost rather take a sharp stick in the eye.

With this thought in mind, I'll be brief. The subject of this book is standing up for what you think is right. And let me say that this point, I know it's not in everyone's personality to stand up, and that's okay. I know there are those who choose to avoid confrontation no matter what. And to be honest these people will most likely go through life better liked, more popular, and perceived as easier to get along with than those of us with this characteristic for standing up. But we both have our place of service. It takes many parts to make up a complete body, and all the parts play a role. This book is to those who have been chosen to stand up, and it speaks to the refinement of this characteristic. It is a characteristic that is often viewed as admirable. It is something that we as Christians are expected to do. But in reality when the role is exercised it is often thought of as being a lot of trouble. It could be considered a rocking of the boat.

I hope this book will offer some encouragement to those who choose or are called to be the ones who stand up. I hope it will inspire the readers to try and refine and nurture this trait in their personalities. We should never attempt to ignore or extinguish these urges to stand up but we should also learn to resist the urge to be overbearing and ready to criticize too quickly. It is not really a matter for these people of just doing the right thing; it is a matter of doing it for the right reason and appealing to a higher motive. These are the motives we should aspire to. It is a compulsion in our personality that drives us, won't let us rest, and motivates us to stand up against what we perceive as an injustice or something that is just not right.

That all sounds very admirable, however, in the real world someone with the stand-up trait that has not refined it or matured in it can just be the guy everyone hates to see coming. I have found myself in this place in my life. It was a place where I would look for a reason to stand up for something, against something, to someone, for someone, or anything just to stand up. Most people, and rightly so, would not view this as standing up, but instead as being outspoken or hotheaded. Knowing what I have now come to understand, I view it as just immature.

Being where I am now, I can look back and see where I might have been a little more subtle and a little more refined. Now at fifty-one years, I can see where I am at and where I have been, and I can look forward to the road ahead.

I was put in a place in my life where I realized that I am the guy who always is required to stand up. I look back at all the standing up I've done over the years. Sometimes it was with the right motives, and sometimes with the wrong. It has taken me years to learn how to apply it in the correct manner.

In no way do I presume to have it perfected. I am still learning. However, learning that I have a lot to learn has brought me a long way. It has brought me all the way from hotheaded, uneducated redneck to a polite, uneducated redneck.

Some would say I have no business trying to write a book. I have had no formal education. True, but I have lived for fifty-one years. I have been married for thirty-one years to a beautiful saint of a woman. I've raised a wonderful daughter who is twenty-seven years old and who is married to an amazing, hard-working, loyal husband who I am proud to call son-in-law. They've produced what I like to refer to as the perfect grandson. This little guy coming along has taken me to a new level of understanding love. I guess you could say that I've been educated by life. I have a degree from the school of hard knocks.

So I admit, I don't posses a formal education. However, I do posses an education from life. I have learned many things the hard way. But I have learned this one thing that's most important: God is my rock; he is my shelter. In him alone I find refuge. Whatever I do, whatever feat I choose to undertake, I undertake it for his glory, his honor.

So I move forward with this endeavor with that as my banner. To God be the glory.

I have also learned that there is no limit to the places God will take a man. I would never have imagined the blessings he has placed in my life. I consider the inspiration to pen these words just another blessing he has granted me.

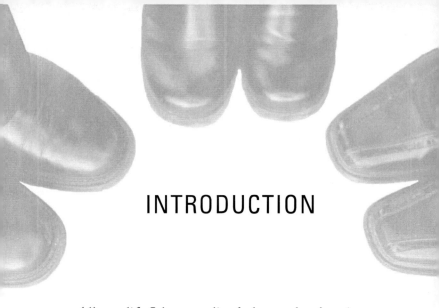

INTRODUCTION

All my life I have realized the truth when it was presented to me. I also recognize untruth, immediately. I know that my spiritual gift is discernment, which is not always a gift that is appreciated. Nevertheless, it is what I posses, and learning to use it for the uplifting of the church is my calling. It doesn't seem to make sense to me to posses this gift and not put it to use. No one wants to be told that they're wrong, so sometimes exercising this gift, if not careful, will not win a person any friends. However, I do not believe that the Holy Spirit would endow someone with a particular gift if it could not be of benefit to the body of believers. So learning to use this gift with discretion and love seems to me to be what it's all about. I feel as though I have made great strides in this area. There was a time in my life that I would not think twice about making my point no matter who suffered for it. But I have learned that just knowing right from wrong is only half of the gift.

When reading the Word it is easy to just hear what we want to hear sometimes. The part that I overlooked for years is the understanding that all the gifts must work together to make the church complete. Insulting someone who does not understand things the way I do, I have determined, is not making the body of believers complete. I believe that aspiring to a higher motive when standing up for what I believe in and not coming across as just knowing something everyone else does not is a better approach. I feel that in this book I make that point clear. I hope that readers will be encouraged in their effort to improve their gift. Whether the gift is discerning spirits or mercy, teaching or healing, they will feel lead to exercise the gift and use it to make the body of believers that they belong to more complete. Whatever the readers' gifts, I feel after reading these words they will better understand this one, that discerning between right and wrong means nothing if we are not prepared to act upon it. We must be prepared to stand up for what we know is right and do it in the right way.

STAND UP:
WALKING UPRIGHT

What can I tell someone about standing up? All we ever hear on the subject is that we need to do more of it. It sounds like an admirable quality to have. Yet it can take you to a place of few friends and loneliness. But for some, even I, this is the place we are bound. To remain silent on a matter that is clearly wrong, though popular, is seemingly harder to do than simply shutting one's mouth.

When standing against an obvious moral wrong like abortion, we are praised by our peers. When standing in front of our Christian brothers and sisters and speaking out for prayer in schools, we are admired. However, stand up in a deacons meeting in front of ten fellow deacons, and you are simply a troublemaker with your own agenda.

Why are some people made to bring this burden upon themselves? Why do we place the "right thing" above our comfort and ease? To say it is "because that is how God made me," is true but not enough. I want to know why it keeps me awake at night. I want to know why I feel this overwhelming compulsion to stand up, even when my wife Sarah, who is an absolute angel and will go completely out of her way to keep from offending someone, cringes when I open my mouth in our Sunday school class.

I don't know how long the line of stander-uppers is in my family history, but I do know that my mom suffers from the same affliction. She stands up with reckless abandon. She would stop a bank robbery in progress if one of the robbers used foul language.

When I was thirteen or fourteen years old, we had some neighbors who had a fight one night. It was between the husband and the wife's brother. In the midst of the dispute, the brother produced a hand gun and the police were called. As concerned neighbors, or nosey depending on your viewpoint, we went over to see what the problem was. Upon arriving on the scene, the brother came storming out of the house with a few choice words for his combatant. My mom froze us all in our tracks with "Hey son, you'd better watch your mouth." It froze him in his tracks too. My mom never slowed down. She walked right on by and into the house with her brood right behind her. After the initial shock at her brassiness, and surveying how everyone took notice, I felt a pride in my family. Without regard for consequences, someone had been courageous enough to stand up for what was right. My mom. With head held high and my chest poked out, I glided right by the would-be criminal with a righteous pride in knowing that justice had been served. There was no cussing in front of my mom.

It is a good thing she never was around with my buddies and me when we were riding bikes home from school and cussing like sailors. But that is another story. The point is, she disregarded comfort to do what was right. The brother should not have been acting like that; he was clearly in the wrong and everyone there, from his family to the police, knew it. However, it took a hundred-pound woman from across the road, armed with nothing more than morals, courage, and common sense, to stand up and say what needed to be said. And she thought nothing of it.

So I guess I get it honestly. It was handed down to me through birth. Blessing or curse, I got it. I think the thing to do would be to groom it, trim the wild hairs off of it, and make it a little more presentable. I've decided that I would try to evolve this characteristic into something more effective.

It is obvious that our society lacks this quality by the state we find ourselves in. Our citizens won't even stand up in the voting booth and are there alone. They won't stand up and take responsibility for their own lives. They allow themselves to be bought by politicians with promises of entitlement programs and not having to deal with the responsibly of taking care of themselves and their families.

If standing up is what I'm called to do, I can honestly say that I've had plenty of opportunities to exercise my calling lately. As I was telling a friend of mine just the other day, I'm tired. I am tired of the loneliness standing up brings. I am tired of the rehearsed monologs I know I will have to recite. I am tired of the stupid decisions I see made because of either a lack of common sense or a lack of courage to stand up.

I have a friend who I trust completely. He is a man who stands up. He stands up in his home. He stands up in running his business. He stands up in his community. He stands up in his role as deacon in his church. He told me this story and how, by his one act of listening for God's voice and not being afraid to stand up, he impacted our entire community.

It was 1994 when he and his family moved into our community from another part of the county. It did not take them long to find a church and to feel God's call there. They were made to feel right at home. After several months of getting involved, he learned of the efforts and struggles the church had been facing in getting their building program off the ground. This was a small country church that averaged about one hundred people in the worship service on Sunday mornings. No matter what they did in trying to get a new building going, the efforts fell flat. They were watching the population of the community explode around them but could not seem to expand their church. My friend then started to realize what the problem was. The church had no leadership. In a church of that size the leadership role lays directly and solely with the pastor. This pastor chose not to lead the people but to drive the people. It was clearly not working. My friend asked a deacon one Sunday, "Don't these people see what the problem is?"

The deacon's response was, "Yes, they see, but no one is going to do anything about it."

It was more than my friend could stand. He said he knew at that moment why God had lead him there. Since he was also a deacon, he brought it up at the next meeting. His words were "It is time that this preacher goes."

To his surprise everyone said "Yes, you are right."

Now when my friend chose to stand up he had no idea that his words would be met with such agreement. He thought he'd have a fight on his hands. To stand up on this subject of running off a preacher who had been at this church for years, as someone who had been there for about one year, was astoundingly bold. But he knew what was right. Everyone else did too, but they chose to stay seated. The preacher was let go, and the search began for the new pastor. An interim pastor came in and did a wonderful job of healing the wounds that a sudden change like this is bound to cause.

It did not take long, about a year, and a new pastor was found. The building program was soon on its feet, and the church grew by leaps and bounds. Two new buildings were built, and further growth is coming. The size of the congregation has more than doubled, and many continue to be lead to the Lord. The community has had a positive impact because one man chose to stand up on a tough subject that had been avoided for years.

I try and remind myself of this particular story whenever I face a situation where I know it will be tough to stand. I remind my self of the victory my friends standing up brought. Not victory for him personally but victory for Christ's church. Even the preacher that was let go has moved on to bigger and better things for the Lord.

Did he do this for recognition or popularity? No, truth be known, he would have probably wanted someone else to bring up the subject at the deacons meeting. But it was on his conscious. So he stood up. End of story.

STANDING IS NOT
RIGHT FOR EVERYONE

There are many books on the subject of standing up for what you believe in. They encourage us to do so. They try to teach the reader the mechanics of the process. They might teach the way to do it effectively and efficiently. I'm thankful for the people who write these books and their effort to try to pursued the masses to join in and make our world a better place. No matter how educated you are on a subject, it's always helpful to hear or read someone else's perspective.

But encouraging someone to stand up, although I think more of us should, is not what this book is about. Although that may be just the purpose it ends up achieving. I'm writing this book for those of us who can't seem to keep ourselves from standing up; I hope to encourage us to pay more attention to the manner in which we do it by seeking out ways to defend and promote the issues that affect our lives and further our purpose without destroying relationships in the process. To try to persuade and convince people, not demand and drive them, is my intention here.

I said all that to say this: not everyone is meant to stand up. Some people, truth be known, should not. Some people can open their mouths with all sincerity and, in just a couple of sentences, absolutely destroy any hope of furthering their cause. We are all gifted, or cursed depending on your perspective, with something in our personalities that's unique to us. The secret is to find out what that unique trait is and do your best with it. Fine tune it, polish it, and take it out and use it when the need arises.

But first we must understand our purpose. I believe we all have the same purpose. Our purpose is to give and to serve. It takes a lot of different qualities to meet all the needs of our world. We all give and serve in different ways. I don't believe that anyone's gift for service is more important, overall, than anyone else's. The importance of the gift is realized in the timing of its application. Realizing the need for the gift and the skill with which it is applied is what brings out the importance of the gift.

Now those of us with the gift of being able to stand up to adversity seem to not only stand up but to also stand out. It may bring more immediate attention to us, but no less important is the one who is gifted with the ability to show mercy and kindness. We should all be able to show these qualities, mercy and kindness, but some people are simply gifted at it. This is my wife, Sarah; she is gifted with the qualities of showing mercy and kindness. We have been married for thirty-one years. In those years she has had plenty of opportunity to exercise her gift in dealing with me. Living with someone who feels the need to stand up and has not learned to restrain it until needed, has to be tough. In my less mature days, I know that I was a handful to be with. I thank God for gifting Sarah with these special qualities. For someone like me to find someone like Sarah to marry is truly a gift. The few in our world, like my Sarah, who possess these traits, are blessed gifts to everyone that they are involved with, but they are not made to be stander uppers.

The same goes for those who may be gifted at administration or those who are gifted at being able to help others. I have a friend who would absolutely lie down and be run over with a truck instead of debating an issue. However, if there is a project that has been undertaken and it requires work to accomplish it, he's your guy. I would describe this guy as gifted at helping others. Our particular body of believers needs him. He makes our congregation complete. What ever the gift or talent, we all have a place of service.

Don't think too highly of yourself if you are a stander upper. A world full of us would not be a pleasant place to live. Not everyone is meant to stand up. Thank goodness and thank God that he made people like my Sarah, with her special gifts, my friend who is not scared of work, the prayer warriors, and the administrators. I thank Him for all the parts of our body of believers that are different from me.

STANDING UP
IN MY YOUTH

When someone is made from his youth to be the one who stands up, youth can be a difficult time. Not that this person cannot have a happy childhood. But it can be trying. The challenges he faces may come from the bully in school or even a rough teacher. Although most would try to avoid any confrontation with these challenging individuals, the stand-up guy is seemingly drawn to them. He is compelled to right their bad attitude although it is probably not the smartest thing to do. It is discernment and discretion the youthful one lacks. Even in the best of cases it takes years of maturity to learn to polish these skills. For me it took about forty years, and nearly twelve years later, they still don't shine like they should.

When I was thirteen, my parents moved to a different town. This meant a new school for me. It was a positive thing in my life. I did not realize it at the time, but my future wife's family was making the same move.

I found the new school to be a very friendly place, but there was this one guy who everyone had to avoid. I'll call this guy Bob. All I heard was how mean Bob was and how tough Bob was. "You'd better stay out of Bob's way." Well, all this talk about Bob just made me all the more eager to meet him. And meet him I did. Now let me say right here that had I been a more mature and discerning stand-up guy, I would have avoided Bob and let life put him in his place. But being on the opposite side of maturity and completely void of discernment, I chose to meet Bob with a complete lack of discretion. My first encounter with Bob was my fist in his face. About two seconds later, I got Bob's response, *his* fist in *my* face. After a few agonizing minuets of responding to each other, it dawned on me, "maybe Bob is a stand-up guy too."

Our first encounter ended as abruptly as it had begun, with a teacher grabbing us both by the back of the neck and dragging us to the principal's office. To my surprise, I learned that day that the principal was a stand-up guy as well. He stood up to Bob and I both with a one-by-four drilled full of holes placed swiftly across our butts. That made me stand up abruptly from the bent over position he had ordered me to take. Paddlings in those days were common place. Today it would mean a certain lawsuit. And they were reserved solely for the boys. I never heard of a girl getting a paddling.

Now you would think that would have taught me that there was a better way to do things. But did it? No. This sort of behavior continued throughout my school years.

I got along with just about everyone, but when that one guy would come along with a chip on his shoulder, I felt like it was my job to knock it off. And let me say that being small in stature sometimes made this job somewhat interesting. Nevertheless, it seemed it was my responsibility to be the one to teach this guy a lesson on how to act. In reality it was me who needed to learn.

I survived those years and actually have fond memories of my high school days. If I could go back, would I do some things different? Of course I would. But doing it the way I did has taught me a great lesson. When I stand up I should stand up for a principle and not against one. I don't have to dislike the person I'm standing up to, and after I make my point, we can go our separate ways and not dread seeing each other again. I have learned to try to forgive others for their mistakes just as God has forgiven me. I have learned that His grace truly is sufficient.

One could make the argument that the stand-up trait in someone without maturity and discernment could be perceived as simply being hotheaded, rude, or even destructive. And I might agree. But people with the trait know in their hearts what they are trying to accomplish. They may not fully understand how to come across, but they know right from wrong. They also seem to value common sense over education and honesty over agenda. They seem to be able to boil things down to the root cause of whatever situation they find themselves in or are addressing.

The stand-up person needs to learn to look closely at what he or she is about to stand up for. True, they know if a wrong is being, or about to be, committed, but they need to be sure that they are not about to sabotage their cause with offensive speech or an improper attitude. I know, personally, sometimes I let my talent for arguing take control of the conversation, and I loose my focus on the true issue.

For most people these things take time and experience to fully master. A few toes will be stepped on over the years while grooming one's skills. The secret is to keep the toe-stomping to a minimum and to maybe learn to avoid it altogether. I've learned that toe-stomping is really nothing more, in most cases, than ego-stroking. An ego can be an unwanted side effect of the stand-up trait. The quicker it is subdued, the quicker the person can get on with growing. But holding on to the whims of the ego can hinder ones journey to a better life. An unharnessed ego can even be a major stumbling block to ones relationship with God. Remember the words of James, he said in James 1:19 that "everyone should be quick to listen, slow to speak and slow to become angry." In other words, shut up and listen and don't be a hothead.

STANDING UP
AND THE FAMILY

People are and should be more relaxed at home. Because of this the stand-up person, if not careful, can cause serious harm. Because of the relaxed environment that the family offers, he or she might tend to let down all restraint and feel compelled to stand up on every decision that is made in the household. In reality everyone needs to contribute.

I have learned to stay out of things that I know my wife is better at. Being a contractor by trade, I have built many houses over my thirty-three years in the construction business. I have dealt with couples that have been at each other's throats from the time we break ground. I don't fully understand why it has to be so stressful for them. Sarah and I are in our fourth house over our thirty-one years of marriage, and not one has ever caused anything but excitement for us. True, by the time we are finished we are tired and ready to see the work come to an end, but it has never caused any problems between us.

However, when building a house this is not always the case. I guess in a marriage there is always one of the partners who feels the need to stand up more than the other. Building a house seems to give them their opportunity. Sometimes I feel that I'm not only a builder but a marriage counselor as well. And believe me when I say I'm not qualified. When the one, be it husband or wife, feels the need to stand up to their partner right in front of me and say "that window need to be two inches bigger" or "that door is in the wrong place" in a tone that is clearly not trying to be constructive, but rather just wanting to be heard, I feel my urge to stand up coming to the surface. Sometimes it's all I can do to keep my mouth shut. But over the years I have learned to keep the reigns tight in these situations. I have actually let some things go that I knew the homeowner would regret later, but because of the intensity with which they argue their point with their partner I decide to remain silent. After all, it's their house, and they will learn in the end.

It would be different if the decision affected others outside their family. I would never remain silent if by doing so my family, church, or business would be damaged in some way.

I built a house for one couple that found something new to stand up for every day as soon as they set foot on the job. They were arguing about light fixtures on the day we started framing the house. They were just arguing for the sake of arguing.

Sometimes standing up in our families is just a little too easy. We are a little too relaxed. I have chosen instead to try to impress my wife every day with kindness. I try not to feel the need to stand up on every subject that I feel is not correct. I have decided to weigh the situation and decide whether or not it is important enough to give my opposing opinion, even if I may not agree with what she is doing. I guess you could say I am not standing up for my point of view; I am standing up for the growth of my marriage. This, in my opinion, is standing up for the higher motive. Let's be careful in our families and not be too relaxed.

I have a friend who was telling me about his relationship with his parents. He said that everyone who knew his family would think that they were the Cleavers. To everyone outside the family they seemed normal in every way. They were church-goers who were hard-working, outgoing, and involved in their community. But he said from within the family nothing could be further from the truth. My friend said that his family was as dysfunctional as any he knew. It seems that in his family there were stander-uppers that refused to grow up. They refused to see that this trait in their personality might possibly be used in a positive way and not lash out at family members to scratch some itch in their egos. In fact the years seem to make things worse. Words became weapons and attitudes became ammunition. I thought to myself as he told his story, how sad that these people were missing what could and should be the best time in their lives. Grandchildren and great-grandchildren and the happiness that they bring are all being missed because members of the same family can't seem to extend the same courtesy to each other that they extend to casual acquaintances or even strangers.

I had no idea how to console my friend, although I know exactly what the problem is. It is people who, like me, have this stand-up type of personality, but unlike me, have decided not to try to grow it into something productive. Instead they let it be a "toe-stomper" and a "bridge-burner" and then wonder why their family is the way it is. I would never say this to him, although if he does me the favor of buying this book, he will soon learn how I feel. What I can offer him is my sincere prayers and remind him to not take the closeness and relaxed environment of the family for granted.

TIRED
FROM STANDING

You would think that standing up for what is right or for a good cause would be energizing. And I guess it is for the moment. It's kind of like an energy rush. But when that rush is over the fatigue sets in. Mind and body are tired. Even just considering the coming event of having to stand up can make you tired. With this in mind, it's not a good idea to dwell on the subject too much. Consider the subject for a time, collect your thoughts, and move on. When the time comes you will be ready. Too much anticipation will wear you out. It will take away your motivation. You can revisit the subject periodically but do not stay on it too long. Stay on it just enough to keep your thoughts and references clear.

Being the stand-up person is to be an asset to the greater good. This includes your family. Tired and burned out, you're no good to anyone, so try to keep a balance.

Sometimes it's as though I have three or four things going at the same time that all require my standing up. These times can seem overwhelming. But, I feel I must endure, keep my eyes on what's right, and stand up for it. I must try to understand that my family and friends, who are not involved in the situation that I've chosen to stand up in, need me too. So my attitude must remain correct for them. It's a hard row to hoe, this standing up thing. But for us who are called to it we have only one choice, do what's right.

There have been times in my life when I would no more than have one trial taken care of than another would move right in to take its place. The best examples in my life always seem to come from church. Church is a big part of my family's life and seeing things done right is very important. It can sometimes create quite a burden. Owning my own business also offers it's own set of challenges but the decisions there rest solely with me which makes things a lot easier but it can still produce a stressful environment. Although I strive to show kindness and compassion to all those I'm responsible to and for, church requires a greater level of these traits. At my job I would rather things work them selves out if possible. But dealing with the different personalities, which are present in all encounters, of my employees and my customers sometimes requires my intervention. When I must intervene I do it with out reservation or mixed words but always with respect of the person I am dealing with. I am confident in my decision to address the matter what ever it may be. However being confident in my ability to say what needs to be said doesn't seem to make it any less stressful.

Same goes for situations at church. Being on the right side of an issue doesn't always make it easy. We also have to keep in mind that at church we are *not the boss*. There comes a point when you will feel, wore out and tired from it all. No one ever said that standing up and doing the right thing would be easy. Sometimes the lingering weight of an encounter is still sitting on your shoulders when the next challenge presents itself. Although tired and desiring peace with everyone, you must continue to stand.

I recall a deacons meeting when a topic was being discussed with passionate views on both sides. The debate rallied on for over two hours. When it was finally brought to an end the next order of business read. It was a controversial topic that the sponsor of which knew would be met with resistance. Upon its being read as new business the sponsoring party suggested that it be "tabled till a future meeting." I knew instantly the reason he tabled the topic and I actually took it as a compliment. My fellow deacon, whom I love and respect, knew that I would be against the idea and although tired from the previous debate he also knew I would again rise to the occasion. The topic has never come up again.

People have come to know of my resolve and the desire I possess to see conservative ideals upheld. Even when we are tired and battered, we must remain on our feet and on our guard.

DIFFICULT PLACES
TO STAND UP

As I grow older, and hopefully wiser, I learn that sometimes it takes as much courage to stay seated with my mouth shut as it takes to stand up. Some things are just me and my ego wanting to be heard. Some are more noble motives. Discerning between the two is where wisdom enters in.

I am a news addict. I love to watch the world news. At my job I love to talk about the news. But in doing so I hear a lot of liberal views and opinions that I don't agree with. Sometimes it's very difficult not to stand up and be honest with whoever it is that I'm talking with. There was a time that I would never miss an opportunity to do just that. But age and the wisdom it has brought have taught me that sometimes it's just not worth it. Sometimes you just have to admit that you're not going to change anything. Although later you may be able to say "I told you so." But that's just that ego trait making an appearance again. I guess the place I find this most difficult is on the subjects of politics and religion. In these I am very conservative and very closed-minded. I heard someone say once that "it's okay to be closed-minded as long as you're always right." However, sometimes being right and close-minded requires that you keep a closed mouth, especially when you are dealing with family or coworkers or anyone else that you interact with on a regular basis.

Sometimes around new acquaintances it can be a little difficult to stand up without fear of damaging the new relationship, unless the subject being discussed turns to something more important than the relationship itself.

If someone I just met prefers vanilla ice cream over chocolate and I am a chocolate fan, and this person wants to make sure that the entire audience knows the superior attributes that vanilla holds over chocolate, then no big deal. I'll let them rattle on for as long as they like, all the while enjoying my chocolate ice cream. But if that same new acquaintance chooses to attack my morals, family beliefs, or my God, then up I'll stand. I'll be quick to make sure that this person knows exactly where our relationship and our opinions are in disagreement. I will not be ashamed of or perceived as weak on my beliefs. Although I would choose not to, my new acquaintance might be offended if he chooses to attack my beliefs. I would try not to use offensive words, only the truth as I see it. Martin Luther said, "Peace if possible, but truth at all cost."[1] I believe that only if the matter is worth it.

It's true that chocolate ice cream is better than vanilla, but it's not worth fighting over. My Lord is sovereign God; that's worth dying for. Once I have decided to take a stand on a situation or subject like this, I can't imagine backing off from it or sitting back down. But I do recall a Bible verse that makes me take exception to the previous statement. The NIV Bible states in Matthew 7:6 "Do not throw your pearls to pigs." Loosely interpreted, I believe that could also read, "Don't argue with an idiot."

Sometimes standing up for your country can be difficult. It's not the standing up that's so difficult but more the being noticed standing that's the hard part. Standing in the voting booth is admirable, and should be done. It is a right that everyone should take advantage of. But it is a slow process. Calling and e-mailing your representatives is a good idea, but it is sometimes hard to see results. Rallies and protest get attention, but do they really work? Still making the effort to stand up is what we are called to do. So, if you feel led to stand up, then stand up. If enough people feel as you do and show your courage, someone will notice.

Another example comes to mind of a difficult situation to stand up in. When I was younger, I had a friend who was a policeman in our town. He offered to let me ride along with him from time to time. I enjoyed doing this on occasion, even though my wife, Sarah, protested. She was very uncomfortable with me doing this and made her concerns known to me. I did it anyway. I enjoyed it without regard to the jeopardy it placed my family in with the risk of my being injured.

I eventually outgrew the desire to participate in this activity and everything was fine. But the stories

I told and the excitement I had for it seem to catch the attention of my daughter. Little did I realize that my selfishness would come back to haunt me. A good twenty years had past and one day, out of the blue, she informs her mother and I that she has scheduled a ride along with the sheriff's department in a neighboring county. She boldly tells us that she has lined up the event. The paper work has been filled out, a date set, and she is raring to go. I was getting a taste of what my wife must have felt twenty years earlier, and it made me feel sick.

I realize now that back when I participated in this activity, against the wishes of my wife, I was standing up for what I wanted to do. That's an example of standing up for ego and it came back to haunt me. I'm glad my daughter got it out of her system.

I believed that doing a ride along with the sheriff's deputy was the wrong thing for my daughter to do, but I still found it a very difficult place to stand up since I had done the same thing and exhibited such enthusiasm for it. Nevertheless, I stood up. She still did it but she had no disillusions about where I stood on the matter.

STANDING UP IN
A SMALL GROUP

Standing up in a small group can be tough. It first of all makes you a very easy target. It can make you very unpopular. It may even make you disliked. But if you are standing up for what's right and not for ego, then stand up you must.

I had this opportunity just a few days ago. Fortunately I knew ahead of time that I would be required to stand up. I had about a week to collect my thoughts. I did not look forward to what was ahead of me. But to stay seated on this matter would have been, to me anyway, to let the name of

Christ go battered and beaten and undefended. No way!

The meeting started out with one of the members praising the group and how well we all worked together. He told what a pleasure it was to attend these meetings. All the while my thoughts, as the accolades were being dished up, were that my fellow attendees had taken the time as I had to collect their thoughts as well. The speaker seemed to be trying to make my chair a little easier to stay seated in and a little harder to stand up out of. I must admit, to a degree, it was working. The thoughts were racing through my head "just let it go." At that moment all I could think of was simply getting through the meeting with a smile on my face and a pat on the back for everyone. But all of us afflicted with the stand-up trait know that's not going to happen.

As soon as the old business was read and the subject of my concern was brought up, all those thoughts of retreat vanished. My mind became focused on my mission but also focused on making sure my ego had been subdued. I did not want this nasty little thing, ego, to undermine my goal. So, I thought to myself, first things first. I quickly lifted up a silent prayer. I asked God for guidance and wisdom. I ask for the correct words and the correct tone. I asked God for my agenda to be locked away and Christ's agenda to be brought to the forefront. I asked for the courage to be bold but not offensive. Reluctantly, I'm ashamed to admit, I asked that if I was wrong on this subject that I be convinced before the meeting is over.

So the debate took off. I let the party with the opposing view speak first. I'm sure, because he knows me, he knew what was coming. However, I'm not sure he was prepared for the passion in which my rebuttal would be delivered.

The debate rallied on for over two hours. At times it seemed to start to elevate and try to become personal. When I felt these urges to let self take control, and maybe lash out with some words that might have made my point very clear but would have been somewhat hurtful to my opponent, I would pull myself back and refocus on my goal, God's will.

Fortunately, and sometimes unfortunately for me, I seem to have a gift for arguing my point. This goes well with the stand-up trait. Although, I have to point out that sometimes I let my ability to argue get in the way of what's most important. I can always feel when the shift takes place from God's will to mine. This is something I'm working on and can say that I'm seeing improvement. The debate I'm describing here, I can say stayed focused on the right thing. Whenever it tried to stray over to "self" it was quickly reeled in and brought back to the correct place. This held true for both sides.

I was pleased to bring this discussion to an end. My points were well taken, and if victory is the correct term, I suppose it was mine.

After the meeting ended my opponent, although I don't like to think of this person by that term, came up to me and told me how he appreciated my passion. He offered no apologies for his position, which I did not expect or need him to do, but praised me for mine. We talked for thirty minutes or more about our commitment to the organization for which we were meeting and our love and sincerity with which we will continue to pursue God's will.

He said that he thought it was a "real good meeting." I was not surprised at this person's positive attitude about things, but I must admit I was surprised at his referring to it as good.

What did I learn from this? I learned that keeping ego out of the debate and having respect for my opponent resulted in a closer friendship when it was all over. It taught me that standing up, when done correctly, can enhance your relationship even with the people you might disagree with, regardless of which side victory might fall.

I'm not going to kid myself and think that my standing up on this matter is over by any means. I will face opposition again and soon. I will continue to stand up. Standing up may not win you any friends, but it may. It may not change the status quo, but it may. It may not change anything that is being done wrong or anything about to be done wrong, but it will without a doubt let those involved know that I stand up for what I believe to be true. Martin Luther said, "You're not only responsible for what you say but also for what you don't say."[2] Amen.

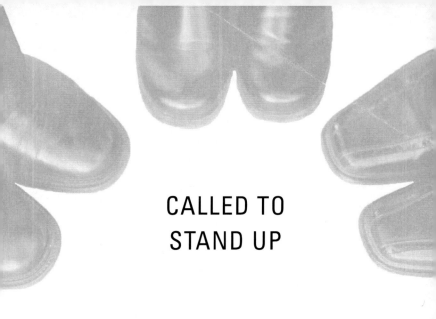

CALLED TO STAND UP

There comes a time when others start to recognize the stand-up trait in you and at times find it to be an asset for their cause. They may come to you and try to persuade you to stand up for them. You will have to determine if you have the same understanding of the issue as the person who is asking for your help.

In the case I will present here, my thoughts and the party that requested my assistance were in perfect alignment. It was the building committee at my church.

We were drawing to a close on the construction of our new fellowship hall. The contractor had done a good job so far and was still within the timeframe he had allotted to complete the job. But the parking lot had not been paved and the rainy season had set in. There had been plenty of time to pave the lot back when it was dry. The paving contractor was telling us that we would have to wait several weeks past the contract date for the lot to be paved. The general contractor offered no encouragement to the paving contractor to get the job done.

Here's where I come in. I was not on the building committee, nor had I been to any of the committee meetings. I did not know the general contractor, and I had not participated in the process in any way. However, a few days prior I had been asked for my opinion on the subject of the parking lot. I thought that since I had been in the construction business for thirty-three years and have built everything from houses to barns to banks, that my expertise was being coveted. It was not. What was being coveted was my uninhibited ability to stand up and say what needed to be said. Everyone at this impromptu meeting that I had been invited to, out of the blue I might add, had the same opinion.

Pave the lot. The general contractor was not at this meeting so another meeting was planned for later that week. It would be attended by the building committee, the general contractor, and his superintendents. My reason for being there became very clear when I went to get in my truck to leave and someone asked me, "Hey Sandy, do you think you could come to the meeting?"

There it was. The reason. The reason I had been invited to the meeting of a committee that I was not a member of, on a project that I had not been involved in. It was not my experience in the construction business that was needed. What was being asked for was the use of my stand-up trait. When the words were spoken "Hey Sandy, do you think you could come to the meeting?" What I heard was, "Hey Sandy, could we use you as a bat to beat the general contractor over the head with?"

And of course I said "okay."

Fast forward to the night of the meeting. We all met in a Sunday school room. In attendance were the general contractor, the building committee, our pastor, and the ringer (that would be me). Our pastor, in his loving and professional manner, started the meeting with an appropriate prayer, then went on to explain our concerns about the paving of the parking lot and the need we had to see the job completed on time. The general contractor had been prepared for this meeting. He immediately started to explain to us about how the paving process works and how long he had been in the building business and blah, blah, blah. What he was trying to do was take control of this meeting. I could feel the hairs on the back of my neck start to stand up. I could feel my pulse beating in my temples. The fact was the time allotted for completion of the project was almost up. There had been ample time to pave the lot. Our view was, "make it happen, stand behind it."

Those were almost the exact words that came from my mouth. There was a moment of silence and then his response. "Well, ok, if you're going to hold my feet to the fire." My response was, "We, (meaning the building committee, of which I was not a member) are responsible for the people of this congregation. They will hold our feet to the fire if this building is not completed on time. So if it's our feet or your feet, guess whose feet are going to get burned?"

His response was "I'll get it done."

And he did. He finished on time and delivered us a beautiful building. We are enjoying it very much.

After the meeting adjourned and I was alone with the building committee, we had a good laugh at the things that were said. I was glad that I could have been of use to them. I love them all and am glad that God has chosen this church to use me and my family. I also must say that I would hire that general contractor to build another project for me or our church without reservation. In the construction business, the best compliment you can pay someone is the compliment of repeat business. This general contractor has my most sincere compliments.

It's fulfilling to me to be to a point where I feel like I have some control over this thing in my life that is so much a part of me. It is wonderful to be able to use it to make a difference for something good and to have other people see it as something that can help to make our body of believers more complete. Everybody has a role to play. It's exciting to know my role, such as it is.

STANDING UP
FOR YOURSELF

You would think that people who have been gifted or afflicted with this stand-up thing that I've been rattling on about would have no problem standing up for themselves. But that's not entirely true. Someone else or some noble cause is easy to stand up for. It is no problem to stand up to someone or some entity that is clearly in the wrong with the way they do business or treat someone. I can stand up and articulate an argument on the spot. But sometimes to stand up for myself takes a little more being abused to get me out of my seat and on my feet. This may be a good thing to a point.

Others should know were you stand, but being humble is every bit as important. Standing up for the moral high ground should not and cannot be compromised. Standing up for the defenseless cannot be overlooked. But greater care and discretion has to be taken when it is yourself you are standing up for. I'm not saying we are to be treated as anyone's doormat, but we should not lord ourselves over anyone either. We are to serve. Service to others is our place of honor. Sometimes serving others is accomplished when we stand up and let others know exactly who we are. Sometimes standing up is done without saying a word.

If we are this person who stands up when called, we must be careful. When standing up we bring attention to ourselves, like it or not. Others must know that although we will not tolerate what we see as injustice, we will stand to the bitter end to see the right thing done; we can also love our adversaries and humble ourselves to the needs of others.

When standing up for yourself, you must be crystal clear about what you believe. Make no apologies for this. Your core beliefs are who you are. You must make sure that you know what you believe. You must be sure of your convictions. How can anyone say they're standing up for themselves if they don't even know who they are or what they believe to be the truth?

I have a bumper sticker on the back of my pick-up truck that reads "I love my wife." If someone asks me about it I do not hesitate to emphasize how much I love my wife. I want people to know this about me. It is a large part of who I am. On the job site I encounter a lot of men who do a lot of complaining about their wives, if they mention them at all. I've encountered men that would read my bumper sticker aloud seeming to think it would some how intimidate me. They quickly learn just how mistaken they are. Without hesitation I will let them, and anyone else within ear shot, know just how much I love my wife and what a blessing from God she has been in my life. I might add that if they have anything less in their lives they need to get to work on it. No apologies.

I will not back down from the things in my life that I have committed myself to. My faith is one of the things that I'm most committed to. I will not allow it to be unnoticed among the people that I interact with. I stand up for Jesus Christ. To hear the Lord's name taken in vain or hear the Christian faith persecuted in some way is something that I cannot or will not tolerate. I take it personally. If someone chooses to talk this way around me they will quickly come to realize that our conversation is about to change in one way or the other. If it's profaning the name of God the person using the foul language will either refrain or the conversation will end, simple as that. If it's bashing the Christian faith then they better get ready to hear my witness. Standing up for myself in this manner, regardless of the persecution I might have to face, is easier than living with myself if I remain silent.

By standing up for my faith I am standing up for who I have decided to be. I have determined that I will keep my conscience clear by not compromising my faith but rather living it totally.

By standing up with my exclamation about my marriage, as expressed on the bumper of my truck, I commit myself to maintain my integrity in other matters while I commute back and forth to wherever it is I'm going. Standing up for myself in this one area of my life, telling my fellow travelers how I feel about my wife and my marriage, has made me a better person in other areas of my life, like my manners behind the wheel. This brings us to the next chapter of this book.

STAY SEATED
WHILE DRIVING

Road rage! It is an amazing condition. I was afflicted with this sickness for many years. I am a recovering "road ragger" and have been road rage free for about five years. I am tempted daily, since my commute is long. I continually have to resist the temptation to bright light someone, tailgate, or mouth the words as I pass someone on the right "speed up you idiot" or "slow down you moron." But in my state of recovery I find it more fulfilling to just let it go. I see other "rageaholics" on the road and it takes me back. They will pull up so close behind me at a red light that I can't even see their head lights. As the light turns green, they launch their car as if at the drag strip. They pass me at the first opportunity, in the turning lane if necessary. I watch their tail lights, as they weave in and out of traffic then fade into the distance. As I pull up to the next traffic light, I stop right beside them. I want to look over and mouth the words, "slow down you moron," but then I recall the state of my recovery and resist the temptation. As the light turns green, I take off again. I think to myself, *I could floor it and make sure this guy can't cut into my lane.* But I remember the bumper sticker on the back of my truck and not only what it says about my love for my wife, but also the integrity that I must display while proclaiming this. For these reasons I choose to stay seated while driving.

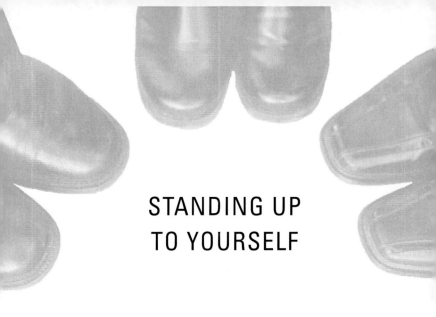

STANDING UP
TO YOURSELF

How does one stand up to his or herself? If you are the stand-up person, and you do not let injustice pass by, haven't you done enough? Isn't it enough to make sure that all those voices that can't be heard, but who know right from wrong, have someone like you speak up for them? You stand up for others, you stand up for yourself, but do you stand up *to* yourself? That's a little different. The initial standing is not so difficult; it's the effort to remain standing that's tough. Allow me to explain.

As I grow older, I know that I need more exercise. I know that I need to get off of the couch and move. "I'm too tired." I know that if I burn energy that my body will reward me with more energy. But to stand up to that desire to sit there is tough.

When I come home from work and want a snack, and there is a bag of potato chips sitting there and some carrot sticks in the refrigerator, self says "eat the chips." But I know what I should do, eat the carrot sticks. When the temptation to sleep a little later or get up early and study my Bible are competing it can be tough. The bed feels great, but I know what I should do. When I'm tempted to "fudge" a little at work by coming in a little late or to take a few extra minutes for lunch or to spend time I'm getting paid for on my personal agenda it doesn't seem like such a big deal. But somebody is getting ripped off. It's not right. I like to think of standing up to myself as a gauge of how much integrity I show.

How well you stand up to yourself can also be gauged by how many things there are in your life that you can say you need to start doing or need to stop doing. Things like "I need to start working out" or "I need to start attending Sunday school." It could be spending more time with my family, turning off the TV during dinner, stop drinking alcohol, and the list goes on and on. Most of the time we just stay seated with our mouths shut. Although quick to stand up and make our point known in situations outside ourselves, we don't correct the issues in our own personalities. And when we do decide that enough is enough we don't stick with it. Not that it's that hard to stand up initially, but it's very hard to stay standing because it requires the effort daily.

To set your alarm clock thirty minutes early and not hit the snooze but put your feet on the floor is a daily battle. To set time every day for Bible study and prayer takes a continual effort. To exercise, to eat and drink with health in mind, and to even spend more quality time with your family takes standing up to your will that some times encourages you to take the low road.

I can honestly say that there are a lot fewer things in my life today that I need to start doing, and it's a good feeling. It's still a daily struggle to keep it going and to try to slip in some new things like not procrastinating and making the contacts I need to make. But when these things pop up in my life and my old self tries to convince me to stay seated, I recognize it as my enemy and attack it.

Every time I stand up to one of these undisciplined characteristics in my life I feel a sense of victory.

When I exercise I feel better both physically and mentally. When I spend my early mornings in Bible study and prayer I feel better prepared for my day. I removed alcohol from my life some time back, and I'm so glad I did. I make no judgments on someone who wants an occasional beer or glass of wine, but I had to be honest with myself; it's not for me. I used to use the old line "it helps me to relax" but speaking strictly for myself, a clear conscience really helps me to relax. And that's what I'm striving for, a clear conscience. No one knows your conscience but you. No one else knows the things you're telling yourself that you need to start doing or you need to stop doing but you. So stand up to yourself and try to be better.

STAND UP
AND BE RESENTED

Although standing up for good and what's right is thought of as being admirable, and those of us who feel compelled to do it know that our motives are to see the truth prevail, it will nevertheless offend someone. Sometimes the offended party will be people who can't see past the noses on their faces. People who, for whatever reason, "just don't get it." These are not the people I'm talking about here, but they are, nevertheless, people we certainly need to pray for. The people I'm talking about here are "the resenters," or the people with a hidden agenda. These people could care less about the truth or what's right. These people will take the opposite side of an issue just because they resent you standing up. They're the ones who will pass you in the hall at work or at the grocery store or even at church and refuse to speak. Just as you are born to stand up they seem to be born to hold a grudge. They seem to be gifted at it. They can hold a grudge over something you say, no matter how sincere or truthful the words. They can be good people otherwise. You would never know otherwise about their affliction. In fact, except for the one being resented, no one else may ever know.

This is what I see as a character flaw in some people. The stand-up trait in you will bring it out. My advice, learn to live with it. Instead of returning their resentment with resentment, return it with kindness. You must still stand up, but outside of the issue you're standing up for, show this person all the kindness and encouragement possible.

No one should resent the truth delivered appropriately. So don't give them any legitimate reason to resent you. Always greet them with kindness and be polite and cordial.

Sometimes these can be highly educated people with lives that seem completely intact. But let someone who stands up for something come around, and they fly all to pieces. I feel that these people feel threatened by anyone with an opposing view point. If they are out-matched in the debate, the resentment gene kicks in. Their only line of defense at that point is to get mad and hold a grudge. I must reluctantly admit that upon discovering I've encountered a "resenter," I enjoy crossing paths with them and being as kind as I can. Always offering a "hello" or "good to see you" even when I know that most likely I'll get no response.

These people can always count on me for these things; I will pray for them, I will always show kindness to them, and regardless of their resentment, I will always stand up for what I believe to be right.

THE MORNING AFTER STANDING UP

As I grow older, and hopefully wiser, I come to realize what this drive in me—to stand up for what I see as right—is really for. I have also come to realize its effect on others. In my earlier years the effect it had on others made no difference to me. If what I had to say to get my point across offended someone, so what. I'd burn a bridge without a second thought. Some of the bridges I've burned over the years have been rebuilt, but it took a lot of effort and a load of humility on my part. Some of the bridges I've burned I'll never have the opportunity to rebuild.

That's my loss. I can see that more maturity earlier in my life could have prevented this.

But here I am now. Thinking that I've learned how to stand up for what I believe to be right and not be offensive to others. I've learned not to intentionally destroy relationships in my life and to be prepared to reach out with a helping hand to all in need regardless of which side of the issue they may be on. This brings us to the subject of this chapter; the morning after. I use to be able to butt heads with someone or some entity on a subject, hack them to pieces, speaking figuratively of course, burn the bridge, and walk away without a thought. I would go to bed that night, sleep like a baby, wake up the next morning, and move on like nothing ever happened. This is no longer the case. Now that I have matured it doesn't work that way any longer. I have learned to try to make my point in as inoffensive manner as my opponent will allow. I try to keep the bridge intact, and be able to shake hands afterward and say "hope to see you again soon." Nevertheless, depending on how much effort the debate required or how much passion about the subject I had to express, I can feel it the next day. I may be wondering if I've offended someone or wondering if I might have stepped on the toes of a resenter. Whatever it is, it makes me tired. I've had situations lately that I could feel the effects from for two or three days. I was tired and worn out, both mentally and physically. I don't know if the fatigue comes from learning the importance of not destroying a relationship and the effort that it sometimes takes to still see justice done, or if it comes from just being older and not being quite as strong as I use to be. Whatever the cause, it keeps me in line, and I'm thankful for it. Knowing how I might feel the next day keeps me on my toes and makes me choose my words a little more carefully. I've learned to nudge people gently, if possible, in the direction I'd have them go instead of ramming into them at full forces.

I can sense the people that I'm associated with or the committees that I might find myself on grow to know me in short order. They know what I'm about and know that I'm not intimidated by adversity. I'm not concerned that this stand-up characteristic in me will not be noticed. It will be. What I find myself most concerned with is that these people know that I respect them and their opinions, and regardless of our differences in opinion, I will not deny them if they are in need and it is within my power to help. After all is said and done we may not be the best of friends, but we certainly do not have to be enemies. Knowing these things, when I leave a stand-up situation I find getting out of bed the next day a lot easier.

STAND UP AND LEAD

I've heard the phrase "we've got too many chiefs and not enough Indians" and although I understand what is meant by this, it is not possible. If we were all "true" leaders there could not be enough of us. Being a "true" leader is more than just being the one who gives the orders. It's more than just being in charge. It's being able to get the most out of the people around you. It's being able to recognize the leadership qualities in those you work with. A true leader is willing to, and will not hesitate to, get down into the trenches with his workers. They'll roll up their sleeves and say "let's get to it." My third grade teacher said something that has stuck with me. She said, "You have to be able to take orders before you can give orders."

How does all this tie in with standing up? If you're going to stand up for a mission or project, then you better be ready to see it through. And don't consider remaining silent on something you know is right just because it requires some work. Be the leader you've been called to be. You had better be ready to implement what you've stood up for if no one else feels led to. You're standing up for an issue and being victorious in the debate. Allowing it to just lay there will surely diminish your creditability.

Some projects take a team effort and cannot be accomplished alone. This is where your leadership qualities will be put to use. If you are standing up for a project that someone else is trying to implement, then be prepared to lend your support. But the point here is, whatever the project or idea, you must be more than just words. You must be willing to act.

The church I attend has a very active "sportsman's ministry." It puts on a grand event every year we call the "sportsman's banquet." It is a very large undertaking. I am the person who suggested our church take on such an event so it stands to reason I am the person asked to be in charge. When the event comes around each year it creates a lot of stress in my life, but it is well rewarded on the night of the event.

My church, Harmony Baptist, is blessed with leaders, true leaders. My friend David is instrumental to me in seeing that this event is a success. He is a leader and is not afraid to roll up his sleeves and get dirty. This is true with just about everyone at my church.

Regardless of what is asked of these people in regards to this banquet, someone will step up and take on the task. From the men who cook the barbeque and stew to the ladies who make the coleslaw and peach cobbler, they all give it their best effort. From the guys who setup the tables to the ones who setup the sound system to the ones who pick up the trash, the church lives up to its name, Harmony.

Being at this place called Harmony makes it easy to stand up for this cause. Having an event like this that will lead people to the Lord is worth all the effort that's required. I wonder how effective it would have been if I had suggested the banquet, argued for it to take place, tried to justify the amount of effort it would require, and then said, "but I don't want to be the one to take it on." If you're going to stand up for a project, then be ready to lead.

We must also be ready to serve others in our role as leaders. When you stand up for other people's ideas or projects that they might bring to the table, you must be ready to not only encourage but to also be willing to "put your back into it." After you have stood up and made your case for someone else's plea or project and helped to make their argument successful, you can't just leave them helpless. You must ask the question "How can I serve?" You must be willing. Sometimes we lead by serving. The person who will, at the beginning, stand up for something and then turn and tuck his tail between his legs when it comes to the work required would be better served to just keep his mouth closed and keep his seat.

STAND UP AND LIVE YOUR FAITH

I'm a Christian. I make no apologies, have no regrets, and am not sorry if it offends you. It's who I am; it's what I am. I fall short of the name in many ways, every day. But I know that I'm forgiven. I know that I have salvation through the shed blood of Jesus Christ. Not because of anything that I've done except to accept Him as my savior. He did the rest. I pray every day that God will guide me and protect my family. And He does. I have faith that He will continue to do so.

I do not choose to bash people over the head with my Bible or stand up every time I hear someone say something I feel is unspiritual. But by the same token, the way someone else acts or speaks is not going to change the way I speak or behave. I will assertively defend my beliefs and convictions and never allow myself to be perceived as passive. All this while trying not to disrespect the offending party. I will try to use words or techniques that hopefully allow the other people to decide in their own minds the mistake in their behavior. I may try, with a carefully placed word or phrase, to plant a seed that will grow into a new characteristic in the person's behavior. It may not sprout until sometime later. It may not sprout at all. But in planting the seed, I've done my job. I've stood up for my faith.

I never miss an opportunity to bring up the subject of my church or something we're doing. This especially holds true at my job site. My employees know without a doubt that I am a Christian. Although they may not all adhere to my beliefs, they respect me enough to not offend me over them. Profanity is kept to a minimum, and I appreciate them for it. Our conversations are always respectful of everyone, and it makes for as pleasant of an environment as can be expected on a construction site.

SANDY MALCOM

Whether or not my crew shares my beliefs, they will admit that the behavior I require of them makes for a better day. Standing up in this environment at first was difficult, but not anymore. Although on occasion I feel the push from someone who's having a bad day to test my commitment to my faith, it is quickly understood that my position has not changed. I'm still standing.

STANDING UP OR
JUST MAKING NOISE

Is there really a time when a subject arises that you can see is going to be decided on, and is going to be decided on the wrong way, but that you should not stand up for? Let's say that there is an issue at church or at work that has been brought to your attention and instantly you know that it's not quite right. Without hesitation you formulate an argument in your mind. You clearly see, in your mind's eye, the flaws in plan before you. As the seconds tick by, you become more and more confident in your thoughts. But now you have to slow down and ask yourself, *is this important enough for me to stand?*

You'll have to decide, *should I speak up or just remain silent?*

Just because you're gifted at debate, and just because you're not afraid to stand up, doesn't mean that your talent is required on every subject. If every time something comes along that you don't agree with you stand up against it, you will become an expected noise. People will start to see you as nothing more than a troublemaker. Discernment is the key, knowing when something is worth the effort and knowing when doing the right thing is more important than the toes you're going to have to step on. Maintain your credibility by not over-using your talent.

If asked point-blank your thoughts on the subject, then by all means, let the truth be known. But there are occasions when harmony in the group is more important.

There is a fellow that I know who is a perfect example of an expected noise. He has something to say about everything. It doesn't matter if it pertains to him or not you are going to get his input. Because of this, no one takes him seriously. He could find a cure for cancer and no one would listen. His out-spoken character has eroded his credibility. It is amazing to me that he is ever invited to any activities or social events. It is not surprising that he is never asked to serve on any boards or committees. My advice to this guy, if ever asked, would be the same advice I've heard an old timer at my church offer many times. He says that "God gave us two ears and one mouth because He wants us to listen twice as much as we talk."

I'm not backing down from any previous statements I've made. The truth is paramount. What I'm talking about here are the little things that in the big picture won't amount to much. I guess you could sum it up as the difference between the things that really make a difference and just having your own way. Standing up for the things that make a difference is standing for the truth; standing up for your own way is simply ego. Until we learn to subdue our egos we will never find true happiness in life. Until we learn to subdue our ego, we need to keep our mouth shut and keep our seat.

STAND UP AND BE RESPONSIBLE: RESPONSIBILITY EQUALS ACCOUNTABILITY

It's not enough to offer leadership; you must offer responsible leadership. Whatever it is that you've decided is worth standing up for and have taken on a leadership role in, you must take responsibility for. You can and should delegate different duties to capable people. This will be a perfect opportunity to discern leadership qualities in those around you. But in the end, if it was you who took a stand for, lobbied for, or argued for a certain thing to be done then consider yourself responsible for it.

Here again, if you are the person who feels compelled to stand up for a new endeavor or program, then you should also be responsible enough to lead the way and see it through to the end.

At the time of this writing there is a news story dominating the headlines that involves an alleged shooter gunning down four police officers while they sat at a restaurant drinking coffee. Before committing this crime, the alleged shooter was allowed to go free on bail after being charged with rape of a twelve-year-old among other charges. As of now the judges who allowed this to happen have not commented.

In 2000, this guy was serving a sentence of over one hundred years. The then governor of Arkansas, Mike Huckabee, chose to reduce this guy's sentence from over one hundred years to less than fifty years. This, for what ever reason, made him eligible for parole. He got out of prison only to return a short time later. Although acting on the advice of people who should know, Huckabee stated on the national news last night, "I am responsible." Upon hearing him say this, I had to do a double take. I could not believe I'd actually heard a politician saying "I'm responsible." But there it was, a politician actually taking responsibility for something that did not go right. In a world of "I did not have sex with that woman" and "it's all the previous administration's fault" to hear the words "I'm responsible" will certainly get your attention. I thank Governor Huckabee for doing the right thing and admitting that he made a mistake. I thank him for standing up and being responsible.

When we choose to take the lead, we choose to take the responsibility.

STAND UP AND
BE POLITE

I find great pleasure in being polite and respectful of the people I encounter. As a result it seems I, for the most part, encounter mostly polite and respectful people. In fact, I really can't remember the last time I came across someone who was not well-mannered, with the exception of the before-mentioned "resenters." I do, on occasion, come across the individual who will always respond to the question "how are you today" with a response like "I'm awful" or "not good." To which I will reply "well maybe the rest of your day will be better." I can promise them that I will do my best to ensure that if they are dealing with me on a matter, I will not add to their awful day. In fact I will do my best to make it a good day from this point forward. I have a friend who always response to the question of "how are you today" with "I'm blessed," I love that. I am committed to a "yes ma'am, no ma'am, yes sir, no sir, let me open the door for you, let you out in traffic, go before me in the checkout line" style of living. I'm also a good tipper.

I can't imagine an activity that I would be involved in when being rude would be necessary. Now I'm not saying that you should be anyone's door mat by any means. But I am saying that everyone should have the opportunity to receive kindness. Kindness should never be mistaken for weakness. In fact, just the opposite—to be able to show kindness is a sign of one's strength. To be polite to all people could be a sign of one's integrity.

I am very competitive and, when challenged, I love to win. But not at the cost of being mean spirited or rude.

My resolve is most often tested when I dine out. Bad service at a restaurant is not acceptable. But it does not require rudeness. I can stand up for myself without being rude. I can get my point across and still be polite about it. The way I'll stand up is to not give that establishment anymore of my business.

In some situations I feel that my frustration must be expressed, but I will exhaust every opportunity for my adversary to know that I'd rather resolve our situation with kind words and mutual respect. I have decided that I will express myself by being kind and polite. The casual acquaintances I make will be left with the impression of having met a nice guy. The people I associate with on a regular basis will have no doubt of my respect for others through my manners. I will stand up and show the courage to be polite.

SHOW INTEGRITY WHEN YOU STAND UP

Being a person of integrity is being a person who is whole or complete, not someone who will say one thing and then do another. The person of integrity will live Monday through Saturday the same way they act at church on Sunday. The person of integrity will go beyond what would be expected of him to make sure to keep his commitments. Being a person of integrity can be very inconvenient. Example: it's 95 degrees outside, I'm dressed for whatever occasion and running late. As I go down the road, I pass a woman with a flat tire on her car. I think you know where this is going. Next thing you know I'm sweaty, dirty, and running even later. There is no way around it. It's just the way some of us are made. I also cannot take a seat when there are women standing. No way, it's not possible. This would also hold true for an elderly man. These are simply small examples of what I view as having integrity. There are many more characteristics that make up the trait. If you possess them, then you know what they are. If you do not possess them, they should be sought out. The giving of yourself in this manner will greatly enrich your life. Learn to be a person of integrity.

Learn to do the right thing even when no one is looking and you may never be recognized for it.

STAND UP
AND BE FREE

Standing up for what we know is right sets us free. When you posses the ability to stand up and convey your thoughts or feelings or viewpoint, it brings a freedom into your life that remaining silent denies. Just to simply have the freedom we have to stand up is valuable. If you are the stand up type and don't take advantage of this freedom, your inaction is inexcusable.

One of the hardest things in life to live with is regret. Why regret not making your voice heard when you have the opportunity? Why have this ability inside of you and not experience the freedom from regret it will produce and not try and not groom it and use it? If someone who is made to stand up does not take the opportunity when it presents itself, it will surely burden this person unnecessarily.

When I know I'm closing in on a situation where my standing up will be required, I spend what time I need in preparing my thoughts. I rehearse in my mind the scenario in which I'll present my case or ideas. There usually comes a point where I'm just ready to get it done. Be it in a meeting of some committee that I might find myself on, or in a situation I must deal with at work. If I let the opportunity come and go and I remain silent when I know I should stand up, it leaves me with a loose end that will keep me bound. I say a loose end because every time I run into the event or thing that I should have stood up to I will know I neglected my responsibility. It will keep me bound by not letting my conscience rest until I make it right. If I address the matter, regardless of the outcome, I am free from it. My conscience is clear. I might not be satisfied with the outcome, but I know I did my job, and I know I lived up to my calling. My associates know where I stand, and I feel free.

JESUS CHRIST THE PERFECT EXAMPLE

If there ever was an example to look to as one who stands up, it would have to be Christ. He even stood up to the Pharisees for what they were thinking. In Luke 5:22 Jesus asked, "Why are you thinking these things in your hearts?" Now that's what I call standing up. He always knew ahead of time that he would have to encounter the testing of his resolve and the testing of his commitment. He never failed. He would be drastically outnumbered and threatened, but he would continue to stand. He knew that it would eventually cost him his life, but he continued to stand. After hearing myself say that, I think of how silly it is for me to be concerned about what someone may think of me when I have to stand up, especially when I have to stand for my faith. When we stand up for our faith in Christ, we are standing for the rock solid example of courage and integrity. It should energize and strengthen us. I'm sickened by the notion that to be a Christian I must be weak and passive. My Christ was anything but weak and passive. He was strong and assertive. I will choose to follow his example. Instead of following like a timid pup, I choose to feel like an empowered warrior with the strength to be kind, polite, respectful, and unwavering in my commitment to display Christ in the way I present myself.

Christ's example of strength was in his ability to stand up and still exhibit love. In 1 Corinthians 13:4–8 we are told what this love consists of. The first thing that we're told is that "love is patient." Then we are told that "love is kind. It does not envy, it does not boast, it is not proud. It is not rude, it is not self-seeking, it is not easily angered, it keeps no record of wrongs. Love does not delight in evil but rejoices *with* the truth. It always protects, always trusts, always hopes, always perseveres. Love never fails." I feel stronger after I simply read those words.

How much more after I put them into practice? I will commit myself to exhibiting this Christ-like characteristic of love in my life.

The account of Jesus' arrest in Matthew is especially insightful to me. At first I would look to the companion of Jesus that drew his sword and hacked off the ear of the servant of the high priest. He stood to defend Jesus even when outnumbered by what Matthew referred to as a "large crowd armed with swords and clubs." That sounds pretty brave to me. However, if I look a little closer, I see the real strength was in Jesus stopping the violence before it went any further and actually healing the injured servant's ear. He healed one of the people who had come to arrest him. To me this is amazing. The Bible does not say, but I wonder how this guy felt—being part of this gang of unbelieving thugs—after Jesus stood to defend him and probably saved his life and then on top of that healed his injury. Was he strong enough to fall to his knees and ask for forgiveness, or so weak that he continued on with his sin? I suspect that if the servant had chosen strength we would have been told of it. After this all of Jesus companions fled and left him there alone with his captors. Jesus still remained standing. They bound him and led him before every authority; they beat him, falsely accused him, imprisoned him, and finally put him to death on a cruel cross. He remained standing. This is what I want my life to be like, unshakable. I am very far from this type of strength in my life, but I will continue to grow. I will continue to stand upright.

IN CLOSING

If you're one of these stand-up people like me, I hope you have come to terms with what you possess. I hope you have learned the do's and don'ts or are at least like me, in the learning process. I hope you haven't stomped on too many toes or burned too many bridges on your journey to where you are now. I hope that growing and learning will be for you a lifelong endeavor with new insights daily.

I hear a lot of people complaining about the aches and pains of growing older, and I must admit that a sore back in the morning or stiff knees after a long ride are not something I cherish. But I would not trade the things I've learned or the wisdom I've gained for another turn at youth. Everyone says, "If

I could go back and do it again, I'd..." But I say that if I could go back and do it again, I'd probably make the same stupid mistakes that I made the first time. I'd live for years with the "I should start" or the "I should stop" things in my life. No thanks on going back. I like it right here. I like it now that I've finally learned who I am and what I am. Who I am is Sandy Malcom, son of Doyle and Joann, husband of Sarah, father of Elise, father-in-law to Slade, and grandfather to Grant. What I am is a follower of Jesus Christ, willing servant, unworthy recipient of Gods grace, and seeker of wisdom. In these matters I find my peace, my happiness, and my freedom. It's a life that gets better every day. I hope and pray that I can share my life lessons with others and they can find their place of service just as I have. This aching inside to stand up for what's right is a gift and we who possess it should treat it as such. We should do the best we can with it and realize that it is for the betterment of those we serve. To give and to serve is everyone's purpose in life. The way some of us accomplish this is by standing up. So if you are the person called to stand up then you should learn to stand up right.

ENDNOTES

1   "Peace if possible, but truth at all cost" Martin Luther. BrainyQuote.com, Xplore Inc, 2010. http://www.brainyquote.com/quotes/authors/m/martin_luther_2. html, accessed July 12, 2010.

2   "You're not only responsible for what you say but also for what you don't say." Martin Luther. BrainyQuote.com, Xplore Inc, 2010. http://www.brainyquote.com/quotes/authors/m/martin_luther_2. html, accessed July 12, 2010. ,